12/94

MISSING PERSONS USA

MISSING PERSONS USA

How to Hunt Down and Find Anyone, Anywhere

ROGER WILLARD

PALADIN PRESS • BOULDER, COLORADO

Missing Persons USA:
How to Hunt Down and Find Anyone, Anywhere
by Roger Willard

Copyright © 1994 by Roger Willard

ISBN 0-87364-771-8
Printed in the United States of America

Published by Paladin Press, a division of
Paladin Enterprises, Inc., P.O. Box 1307,
Boulder, Colorado 80306, USA.
(303) 443-7250

Direct inquiries and/or orders to the above address.

CONTENTS

1 Introduction

5 Chapter 1—A Short Story

9 Chapter 2—Details

13 Chapter 3—Where to Start?

17 Chapter 4—My Favorite and Most Obvious Sources

41 Chapter 5—Things to Think About

45 Chapter 6—When You Are Stumped

49 Chapter 7—Coincidences Do Happen!

51 Chapter 8—State of Mind

55 Conclusion

59 Appendix A—Missing Person Report, Personal Data

69 Appendix B—Request for Change of Address

71 Appendix C—Request for P.O. Box Disclosure

73 Appendix D—Request for Business P.O. Boxholder Information

75 Appendix E—Military Locator Addresses

77 Appendix F—Book Distributors and Publishers

79 Appendix G—Bibliography

It was in November 1973 that I met Charlie George. The following year he took me under his wing, and I became a bounty hunter. From then on, I was hooked on hunting missing persons and began to learn as much as I could about finding people. Charlie taught me a lot, and for this I am grateful. Later our paths would lead us in different directions, but we remain friends and talk frequently. So, in saying all of that, Charlie, this book is dedicated to you.

ACKNOWLEDGMENT

Patti, my wife, first learned of my midnight runs with Charlie George before we were even married. She knew then that life with me would somewhat different and, more so at times, difficult. She married me anyway. Through it all she has helped me in more ways than I could ever count, one being the countless hours she spend proofreading this book for me. So, to Patti, with all my love, thank you.

To the reader, thank you for purchasing this book, but with it comes an obligation to use it in a responsible manner. Though the activities described herein are generally legal and proper, except where stated otherwise, not every state may see it that way. Please be forewarned that it is up you, the reader, to determine whether what you are doing is legal where you live or where you are conducting the activity. Therefore, neither the publisher nor I condone nor encourage the use of the information in this book in any unlawful or wrongful manner.

Why another book about finding missing persons? I probably own or have read practically every book out there on the subject. Besides most of their being good, a few of them also gave me an idea or two. These books will usually give you a long list of sources—addresses for Department of Motor Vehicle (DMV) records, addresses for some government agencies, and so on—plus a few ways to use some of them. This is fine, but after awhile, most of them start looking the same. I found that the same information seemed to be missing in all of them: how to actually find the person you are hunting.

I have tried to not only list some of my favorite and most practical sources but also give ways to use them. Many times I will tell a short story to show you how a source was used while at the same time trying to keep it a little light and somewhat entertaining. I do this because I believe you are more likely to remember a source and how to use it if I make a strong impression. Just listing sources will not do that for you.

I have written this book with the private citizen in mind, although law enforcement agencies can and do use the same techniques. I have not listed sources like National Crime Information Center (NCIC) or INTERPOL because they just are not available to the average private citizen. Think of this as a companion to some other books and a layman's guide to manhunting. Also, it is meant to help you start thinking like an investigator.

REDEFINING MISSING PERSONS

What is a "missing person"? Sometimes I think this may not be the most accurate term to describe such an individual, but it is probably the most widely used. To me, the only persons who are really missing are those like Jimmy Hoffa. The rest usually know where *they* are. In conducting our investigation, it helps to understand why the person is missing. Many times it will guide us in our search for them. Listed below are some of the ways that I sort the types of missing persons I investigate. You may add or delete categories as it best suits your work or your needs.

• *Lost contacts*. The best examples of these are heirs, lost loves, and parents or children who were involved in an adoption. These people are not running from anyone, nor are they deliberately trying to conceal their identity so as not to be found. They do not even know someone is looking for them.

• *Runaways*. Teenagers are the most likely candidates for this group, but sometimes adults are runaways, too. Runaways can be hard to find, depending on the resources they have available to them. A teen with little knowledge of the real world and limited funds is easier to find than the streetwise teen who knows how to manipulate his friends and others he meets. Knowing the amount of planning done by the runner can also help you gauge how difficult your search might be or how far you should set your sights on finding him or her. Obviously, the more planning the runaway has done, the greater the chances that he might have traveled some distance or be well hidden. Little planning might be an indication that the runner stayed close to home or within range of close friends.

• *Debtors.* The skip for financial reasons probably accounts for the largest group of missing persons this investigator has had to deal with. Since debtors are probably the largest group of missing persons, they range from very easy to impossible to find. Again, some of these people may not even know they are being hunted. On the opposite end of the spectrum are those who are on the move constantly because they are consciously trying to avoid being found for financial reasons.

• *Criminals.* Little needs to be said about these, except that I have had cases where some of them did not even know someone was looking for them. That usually happens after several years. They forget that they were wanted or that they were out on bail. They moved, and no one ever bothered to look for them before. This is usually not the case, though. Most of the time, they are doing just about anything to keep from being found. Note that most criminals who have warrants against them are found by sheer luck, usually during a traffic stop when the officer runs a wants-and-warrants check.

• *Witnesses.* A subpoena has a strange effect on some people. Some will do just about anything to avoid being served a subpoena, while others recognize their obligation and accept it with little or no problem. Finding a witness is sometimes a chore in itself. Due to the many delays in court actions or even in filing lawsuits, people move away, not knowing that they might be needed long after an incident occurred—maybe even years later.

It should be noted here that even within these groups, there could be subgroups. These subgroups can and probably will take you in different directions, a point I will discuss later.

There was a purpose for the exercise of sorting and categorizing our subjects. It was designed to provide us with some information about the person for whom we are looking, and that is the key to finding someone.

CHAPTER ONE

A Short Story

The young investigator was eager to impress his supervisor and anxious to show off his abilities when given the assignment of finding an important witness for an old automobile accident. Finally, after several years, the case was being taken seriously by the opposing attorney. Apprentice PI Jim was now told to find the witness and get a statement.

He ran out of the office with his notebook and a copy of the accident report and went to the old address he had been given. He canvassed the neighborhood for clues as to where the witness might be now. Later, he did a search of public records in the courthouse and city hall. He had a source run a DMV check, which finally provided some new information. Again, he made a check with a new neighborhood, and a day and a half later he found the witness. Jim returned to his boss and presented him with the report, beaming with pride at his accomplishment and thinking he was a regular Sherlock Holmes. The supervisor glanced over the report and showed signs of his satisfaction with the content of the witness' statement. After he finished reading it, he looked up at his young protégé and said, "It's a fine report, but I need to ask the witness about one more thing. Do you have his telephone number?" The young apprentice immediately turned around and grabbed the telephone book and in a second replied, "Yes, here it is—555-12 . . ." It took about a second for it to hit him—it was right there in the telephone book all along.

The obvious point here is, why do it the hard way? Don't overlook the obvious. Just because the witness was thought to have moved since the time of the accident didn't mean he was hiding. Don't make it harder than it really is.

BEFORE YOU RUN ALL OVER TOWN

Most of the time you know or have a good idea of whom you are looking for. The exception would be adoption cases. Other than that, most of the time you have at least a name to get you started. But this can be just the beginning of your investigation.

The investigation starts by identifying your subject. You must be certain of the person you are looking for. This doesn't mean just the person's name. Naturally, the name is important, but you must try to get as much information on your subject as possible. If you are doing the search for yourself, one of the best things you can do is sit down at a table and write down everything you know about the person you are hunting, such as his or her date of birth, Social Security number, past addresses, relatives, work situation, and anything else that will give you insight as to who and what that person is.

More than once, people have been found because they were known by a first name and some other obscure fact. Knowing that Bill is the big guy who used to work over at the brickyard might be enough information to tell you if he is the fellow you are trying to find. If you know the Bill you were looking for is small and has only sold insurance for a living, you will know he's not the one. But if your

Bill is a large, heavy guy and has usually worked in construction supply, you may have just found the right man.

If you have been retained by someone to find a missing person, you do the same thing, except you must first pick the client's brain for everything he knows about the subject. You must take the time to try and find out the details. The few extra minutes now will probably save you hours of work later. If you must, push the issue, and keep digging until you are completely satisfied you have every bit of information the client has.

I have done searches for clients in the past where I spent several hours just trying to find out about the subject. I would later discover information that my client already knew but didn't remember or didn't think was that important when we first spoke. In most cases, it would have saved us both time and money if he had just given me that information initially.

Appendix A of this book is a detailed missing person report/personal data form that I sometimes use during an investigation. It's not always necessary, but for the novice or for more difficult cases, it is a good guide to use. Remember, this form is printed on paper, not carved in stone. If you think something should be added or taken out, or the information could be rearranged to better fit your needs, change it.

CHAPTER TWO

DETAILS

Before I was licensed as a private investigator, I worked with someone who taught me how to be a bounty hunter. On one of our cases, we were looking futilely for a man. We didn't believe he was hiding, but rather that he was a drifter and did not keep a regular address or stay in one place for more than several months. The case looked interesting. The subject had skipped bail for DUI and was supposed to have only one leg.

Eventually, I located his ex-wife and called her on the telephone. She was gracious but said that she hadn't heard from the subject in a while, which really suited her. They did have a daughter, she said, and he would sometimes call there to see how she was doing. Another month went by and we still did not have him, but we knew he was somewhere in the state. Finally, we took a day trip up to the small mountain town where his ex-wife lived, and I spoke with her face to face. Again, she was open, but she still did not know the whereabouts of her ex-husband. However, she did say that several months ago he had sent their daughter a gift, but there was no return address on the package. I had asked her if the package gave any indication of what area he might be living in or where it might have come from. She then said, "Well, there was a postmark of the city." She remembered the city, and with that and checking some public records, we found him two days later.

Details are important, but you must learn to separate the good information from the clutter of useless details. Obviously, the fact that there was a postmark on the package was gold to us. The fact that the gift was a set of children's books or a dress would not be that important unless there was a receipt or something special about the gift that would identify where it came from. The fact that the man had one leg helped us when asking questions, because it was something most people remembered when asked whether they had seen him or not. Also, it helped us identify him when we finally found him. Since he had jumped bail on a DUI, we knew there was a good chance he was still a drinker. Still, many times it is the little details that make or break the case.

With computers, the old saying is "junk in, junk out." The same is true with the information you gather on your subject. If you're dealing with bad information going in, your results will probably be just as bad on the way out. One of the things I like to do during the course of one of my investigations is confirm my information on the subject as I go along. If you started with a piece of information that is bogus or only half right, you might never find whom you are looking for. More than once, the names given to me have been spelled wrong. More often, the Social Security numbers or dates of birth were so far off that it looked like my client just picked numbers at random.

The Social Security number and date of birth are probably the most important sets of numbers you will use in your search for your subject. These numbers are for life—or they are supposed to be.

While talking to a source or someone who might have information on the subject, you want to make sure you are talking about the same person. When checking sources or other people, get some identifying information from them on the subject. You might be surprised at how many people have the same name and are about the same age as the person you are searching for. Middle names or initials are important, as are the tags of junior and senior. Maiden names, parents' or children's names, and certain physical features can also help you find the right person or tell you if you are tracking the wrong one.

CHAPTER THREE

WHERE TO START?

Once you have as much information on your subject as possible without actually going out, then the time has come to analyze it all and decide where to start your search. Remember Jim, the apprentice PI who ran all over town? Look for things about the person that will permit you to look for the subject, even without leaving your home or office. Start with the phone book or use directory assistance.

Here's a really big, *obvious* clue for you "soon to be detectives." Think of your investigation not in terms of looking for the person directly, but rather how many other people or sources of information will know where to find the subject. It may seem strange or contradictory at first, but it is easier to find a lot of people than it is just one.

Now, back to what we did in the beginning. The type of case or the person for whom you are looking will help you determine where to start. Several years back I was talking to a local television station about how good I was at finding people and trying to convince the management to feature me on one of their local programs. They challenged me to find three people. They had asked members of their staff to think of people in their past whom they had not seen or heard from in a long time. In each case, the circumstances and the length of time since the subject had last been seen varied.

The first case involved finding an old college chum of one of the station's staff, who knew the approximate time the subject graduated as well as his major. With that, I took what I thought was the obvious route. I called the subject's college and asked for the alumni department. When alumni start living on their own and putting down roots, they usually notify the alumni association of where they are living. In this case, the alumni association had an address for the subject's parents, which is often the case if the student graduated in the last few years. From this point it was just a matter of contacting the parents, and eventually, the subject called.

The second case was a bit more difficult. It involved a boy who had been in the eighth grade with one of the employees. She had his name and the town they had lived in at the time. The problem was that the boy's father was killed in an accident around the same time, and his mother had moved shortly thereafter. The regular DMV sources did not show that either the subject or his mother was still in the state, and there was nothing available by way of directory assistance. Here was a case where I had to go to a different state, to the town where the subject had lived in eighth grade. A search of the local newspaper archives finally shed some light on the case. Almost immediately after his father's death, the remains were flown to his hometown in Georgia. By chance, the church involved in the funeral was the same denomination as mine. I asked a friend in our local congregation if he knew of someone associated with our church in Georgia who might be of help. He just happened to know the right person to get me in touch with the people most involved in the church in the father's hometown. From there, I talked to people who put me in touch with some family members. After that, I received a call from the subject's mother, who put me in touch with the subject.

The final case involved finding the third employee's long-lost sweetheart from second grade. All I had to go on was the subject's name and the private school the two had attended. This was probably the easiest of the three cases. The fact that he'd attended a private school helped, but what was better was that the subject's last name was not all that common.

In my office I have telephone books from all over my home state, as well as ones from a number of major cities across the country. All I had to do was check the name in the phone book in the area where the subject grew up. I found that there were only three people listed with that last name. It only took two more calls to find the subject. What made it a bit easier was that one of the numbers listed was that of a professional—the type who could afford to send his children to a private elementary school. I called that number and reached an office where the person who answered knew the family member for whom I was looking. She called the family's home number and had someone call me back. After I explained whom I was looking for and why, I was given the subject's telephone number. Eventually, the subject contacted me. About two weeks later, I was featured on the local television program, and we surprised the host with a telephone link to his long-lost sweetheart. Up to this time we had not told him that we had found her. (Unfortunately for the host, though, while she could remember that there was a boy in her class with his name, she didn't remember him very well.)

The common lesson in these three cases is that even though they were all lost contacts, the last point of contact guided us to a starting point. In a missing debtor case you would probably need to find out if the subject had any other bad debts and check those sources. A case involving a teenage runaway might require you to spend several hours going through the young person's personal belongings to look for clues as to his or her state of mind and possible destination. With criminals, you may have to learn the art of pretexts (convincing people you are someone you are not so they believe they should give you information) along with the use of as many sources as possible. Note that using pretexts may backfire and may be illegal in some instances as well.

Another big clue for you would-be Sam Spades, if you haven't figured it out for yourselves yet, is that most of the time you don't find the subject directly; you find someone who knows him or her (ex-spouses, relatives, live-ins), who in turn point you to your subject.

CHAPTER FOUR

MY FAVORITE AND MOST OBVIOUS SOURCES

PHONE BOOKS

The telephone book is probably the most overlooked source of information at our fingertips; not just the current ones, but the old ones, too. In my library, I have kept all the old phone books of my hometown over the years. Sometimes an old address is better than none. From there you can go to a neighborhood check. Don't overlook neighboring communities' phone books. Sometimes your subject will end up in a different directory just by moving two miles.

U.S. POST OFFICE

More than once I've paid a few dollars to the U.S. Post Office for a forwarding address. If your subject moved and wanted his mail at his new address, he probably filled out a change-of-address card. This ensures that the post office will forward any mail sent to the former address for at least 1 year. The time period during which many post offices will forward mail has expanded from 1 to 2 years; I have come across some that, for some reason or another, kept change-of-address cards for 3 years. It's rare, but it has happened.

You can obtain the subject's new address from the post office for $3. You will probably find that one change of address will lead you to another at another post office. In the end, it is still well worth the $3 for each change.

If the post office is local, I usually go right there and try to get the information on the spot. When I was serving legal papers or subpoenas, I would let the clerk take a glance at the paper. More than once, he or she would just look up the information and give it to me at no charge.

The Federal Freedom of Information Act gives you the legal right to request the forwarding address of a subject if he has moved. It is not always necessary to quote the law on this, as requests are made so often for different reasons. I have included in Appendix B a copy of a letter I use that works very well for me. It generally provides me with not only the change of address, but other information that is helpful. I usually photocopy the letter and fill in the name and last known address of the person for whom I am looking. On the bottom of the letter is an area for the postmaster of the local post office to fill in the blanks. With the letter, I enclose a check made out to "Postmaster, (Name of City)" and a self-addressed, stamped envelope.

While we are talking about the post office, let's not forget P.O. boxes. When you request a change of address, a P.O. box is treated the same way as a street address. If your subject has moved, you can request the forwarding address. If your subject has a P.O. box, there will be a signature card on file with the street address listed. However, in most cases the post office is not permitted to give you the information off the card.

So what do you do? If you have a P.O. box for an address, and the town is not too large, just walk into the post office and ask where the subject lives without referring to the P.O. box. There are no regulations against people in the post office giving information on what might be common knowledge to them. Several times, when all I've had is a name and a P.O. box, I would go to the local post office and ask if anyone knew where the subject lived. If the name was not familiar to the person at the counter, the clerk would ask some of the carriers or sorters in the back if they knew where the subject lived. With that, the clerk would give me names of streets and landmarks to look for in getting to the subject's house. All this without anyone violating any laws against giving out P.O. box signature card information.

But there is a law that permits the post office to give out P.O. box information. This law permits this information to be given out if it is necessary for legal action and the subject you are looking for is a party to that action or is in some way necessary to any of its proceedings. Again, a copy of a letter used for that purpose appears in the back of this book in Appendix C. Not to say that you won't have problems with this at times, but every time I have gone directly to the post office and showed a clerk the legal papers, I have left with the street address off the signature card.

Another thing about P.O. boxes is that if the person you are looking for operates a business using a P.O. box, the post office is obligated to give you the street address of the business. I would not suggest that you claim your subject is operating a business if it is not true. You should be prepared to prove the person is in business if it is not common knowledge at the post office. A copy of an advertisement or a receipt with the P.O. box listed on it would be good to have on hand or to enclose with a written request. You will find a copy of a letter requesting this information in Appendix D.

DIVORCE RECORDS

This can be one of the greatest sources of information to aid you in your search. One problem, though, is that not all divorce records are considered public record. You have my sympathy if that is the case in your state. But if they are open, as they are in most states, they can give you a wealth of information. Better yet, most of the time, the older the record, the better. Before adultery was decriminalized in most states, there had to be grounds or someone at fault to get a divorce. That usually meant there would be a lot of mud-slinging back and forth and put into the records. I cannot tell you how much or what you will find, but it is sure to be interesting tabloid reading.

Once a 45-year-old divorce record took me to the sister of my subject in an adoption case. Within a few hours I was speaking to my client's natural mother, who shed tears when I told her that her son wanted to meet her. My client told me later that his mother had since passed away, but he was grateful for the time they did have together.

Most of the newer divorce records will not have a great abundance of information, but some key information can still be found. If there are children involved, support and custody information will help point you in the right direction. Most of the newer divorce records will give you the name of a spouse who might be willing to give you some information.

A while back, another PI asked me to find a woman for his client. Apparently the client had left his wife a number of years back and wanted to get married again. He needed to get a divorce from his first wife before he could do that. My friend gave me the basic information about the subject, along with the fact that she may have gone back to her home state. I went to work checking what I thought were all of the quick and obvious sources first, but nothing came up.

I then checked and found out that the state where she might have gone had an office at the capitol dealing strictly with all divorces in that state (not all states have this or make it available as public information). First, I contacted the office by phone. I have found that even though there is a charge to search for the information, some very nice person on the other end will sometimes do a quick check to tell me if there is anything there. This time they just told me to send $5 for each 5 years I wanted searched, along with the subject's and the client's name and any other information I had.

I sent the request, and a few weeks later I got my reply in the mail—two certified copies of the divorce decree. Since the client had abandoned her more than 7 years ago, she had divorced him. This was a double bonus for the client, because not only could he get married as soon as he wanted, he didn't have to pay for a divorce. (I just wondered if the second wife really wanted to marry a man who had abandoned his first wife.)

MARRIAGE RECORDS

As with the divorce records, not all states consider marriage records public information. But if the records are public or "open," they just seem to throw information at you. However, my experience has been that, unlike divorce records, the older marriage records were not always as complete as they are today. The older records listed age instead of date of birth. Addresses were often rural route numbers instead of streets with numbers. Sometimes very little background information was included at all. Most of the time, the more current the records are, the more complete the information about the subject and his or her family background, including dates of birth, addresses of applicants and parents, past marriages or divorces (ex-spouses), location of the ceremony, who officiated, and what trades or professions the two were in or even if they were students at the time. Some or all of this information might help you in one way or another to get to your subject. When looking for a female, this is one of the best places to start, since if she did marry, chances are she changed her name. If the female was married before, it may tell you when and to whom. Don't forget that her parents may still be living, too.

A small booklet that I keep close is *Where to Write for Vital Records*, put out by the U.S. Department of Health and Human Services. It has the DHHS publication number (PHS) 87-1142. You can get it by writing to the Consumer Information Center, Pueblo, CO 81009, and requesting its catalog of publications, then ordering the book through the catalog.

VOTER REGISTRATION

Even if the subject hasn't voted in a while, there may still be information on his signature card that will get you snooping in the right direction. It will list the last time he voted, his address at the time, previous addresses, and when he first registered. Again, you can find the subject's date of birth, signature (to make sure you are looking for the right John Doe), physical description, and even some old addresses.

This is a source that sometimes makes it too easy. There have been cases where all I did was check voter registration to come up with a good address for my subject. When this happens, I almost feel guilty about charging my minimum fee for finding the person.

I said almost. Remember, if you are in business, you have bills, too, and you cannot help anyone if you go broke giving your services away. Besides, like you purchased this book and dedicated the time to educate yourself on these techniques, I had to pay a price for this knowledge. This knowledge permits me to do my work in the quickest and best way possible. My clients know that there is a minimum fee and are willing to pay it because, in the long run, they would probably have to pay a lot more if they went to someone else who could not do it as fast as I could. This is not to say that you cannot cut people a break at times, but you should make it clear that this is an exception and not the rule for your business. Like most private investigators, at times even I get softhearted and waive my minimum. At times you might feel that you should give the information away because your client cannot really afford your service and it really wasn't all that difficult. As a general rule, I will charge something for my services. Anything given away is perceived as having less value and will diminish your value since it came from you. Secondly, your clients will value it more if they know that they paid for the information, no matter how small the amount. And it will help them to maintain a sense of dignity and self-esteem.

ASSESSMENT

A PI friend from the other end of the state called me and asked for a little help. He said he knew the subject he was looking for was somewhere in Los Angeles but didn't know how to find him. There was no telephone listing for him, and he needed to find him quickly. I asked my friend if he thought the subject might have owned property in LA. He said it was possible, if not probable. I told him to call the LA County Tax Office of Land Assessment, or whatever they called it out there. I told my friend that somewhere there would be a tax record if the subject owned property. With that record would be the location of that property and the address where the tax bill is sent (they may be different). I told him to get all of the information he could and call me back. A few days later he called to thank me because he had all of the information he needed and a satisfied client.

Sometimes the tax offices will give you the information over the phone. If not, you might have to request it by mail. I usually go into our local office, flip open a computer printout, and get what I need. Then if it happens to be out in the country and I think finding it might be difficult, I can go to the deeds office and get a photocopy of a map showing exactly where it is.

WILLS

Early in my career as a private investigator, I was asked to find the heirs to an estate. Working with the will and what was known about the named heirs, I started to look at death records and other wills. If you happen to know the names of your subject's parents, you can look to see if either of them has passed away. If there was a will, there will usually be an executor, who may know where the subject is. Better yet, your subject may *be* the executor. If the executor doesn't know where the subject is, there might be someone listed on the will who does. In this particular case, I found all of the heirs. Some of them were deceased, though, so then I had to locate their heirs, too.

MILITARY DISCHARGE

There are two possible ways to get information about someone who was in the military at one time. All of the branches of the military have archival records of where and when someone was dispatched. Along with this they provide a military locator service. They will also show whether or not the person currently has a pension or some other benefit. In Appendix E you will find a list of addresses for each military branch. There is a charge for nonmilitary personnel, so it is best to call ahead to find out the current fees.

Somewhat lesser known to those investigators who were never in the military is that people who are discharged from the military are required to register with the local courthouse in the county where they will be living. In my county, they would register with the Recorder of Deeds. What this has to do with deeds, I have no idea. But that just shows you the logic of government. In your state and county it may—and probably will —be different. If you go to this office for information, you will probably not get any. But sometimes—and I must emphasize *sometimes*—there is information available from these records. Before computers and microfilm, everything was kept on paper. After awhile an office would run out of room for all of its records and transfer some of them to its archives. How long records are kept in the office and then transferred varies from office to office. I have found, though, that if a courthouse has an archive, the records transferred there are usually considered open to the public. Sometimes, just checking to see if the person was in the military gives you something to go on.

CROSS-REFERENCE DIRECTORIES

I really like these books. Across the country there are several companies that publish cross-reference or street directories (sometimes called reverse street directories). First, they list the city; next the streets, alphabetically; then the house numbers in their proper order; and finally the residents. Usually, along with the resident's name, a telephone number and the length of time at the residence are also given. These directories are printed by private companies, which buy the lists from the telephone companies and then publish them in reversed order.

Some directories will list the names of the people in the city, much the same as a regular telephone book, followed by the name of a spouse if there is one; the place and type of employment, whether the person owns or rents, and sometimes, the person's children. Some cities will have several of these directories, and it is a good idea to become familiar with all of them and the kind of information they provide. These companies start with the telephone list but also send out questionnaires and sometimes even canvass door to door in order to update their information.

Where I am located, there is a regular reverse street directory and a reverse telephone directory in one book for the entire county. We also have a directory with a listing by names, then the streets, and finally, a telephone directory in the back. The second type comes in two volumes. One is for the city in my area, and the other is for the outlying communities. Between the three books, you can get a lot of information. As with telephone books, old copies are helpful, too. A past neighbor can be a big help, even if it has been 10 years.

I had a case recently where an attorney needed to find someone in another city but could not find an address for her. He had checked directory assistance, but she was not listed. At my local library, I found a 3-year-old directory of the subject's city that listed her. It turned out that she had divorced but still lived at that address. The telephone was now listed in her son's name. I visited the subject and got what I needed, just because I looked in a book.

I have several past copies of these directories, but I cannot afford to buy one new each year for every city in my area. What I usually do is just call my local library and ask the reference department to look up something for me. If it is a tough case, I just stop in and look it up myself to make sure there are no mistakes. Also, by going into the library you can check and see if what you are looking for is off just by a line or two. I am fortunate in that my library has a number of directories from different cities around the state. If I need information about another city and our local library does not have a cross-reference directory for it, I find that city's library can usually help me. If not, I then try the local chamber of commerce, and most of the time, if a directory was published in that area, it has it and is glad to assist you.

This is probably a good place to mention that cross-reference directory services, along with a number of other search services, are available to those who have computers with modems. I use one service through a local credit bureau, which permits me to have access to some of its services. There are several other companies that offer similar services and can do some of these checks for you, either over the telephone or by modem. Prices do vary per type of search, as does the cost to sign up for the services. If you are going to do a lot of missing persons investigations, it may be to your benefit to sign up with one of these companies. Complete books have been written on how to do investigations by computer or through the use of data banks.

I feel it's important to mention, though, that these services are not a cure-all for your investigations. In one case I had, I probably could not have found the person I was looking for without data banks. Sometimes, though, the information they provide will be nothing new, but you will still have to pay for it. The information is updated only when someone puts it into the system. If the subject hasn't done anything to cause the file to be updated, only the old information is returned. Even if the subject is getting established somewhere, it doesn't mean that information will be put into the system right away. It may take weeks or even months for the system to be updated.

If you have a computer and use a modem, some systems put you in direct contact with a mainframe computer. Other companies' systems work like an electronic mailbox system. You send your request for information, and the system routes it to the appropriate vendor, who will then look up what you want and send it back to you by way of the system. Still others offer even more creative ways for you to use their systems. But I must stress that you should find out what kind of system you are working with and understand it completely. Only this way can you use it for all it's worth.

The data banks that provide nationwide services on record searches usually have stringers in the area where you want the search done who actually go and do the search and then transmit the information back to you. This process may take anywhere from a few hours to more than 24 hours. The time of day and the day of the week may also play an important part in how long it will take. Where you may run into problems is when you need all of the information in a file and the stringers only send you what they think is important. Some of the services offer information most people could not get any other way, and if that is the case, use them.

A word of caution. Some companies will say that they can get anything or any kind of record. Ask yourself, "Does the end justify the means?" If it is important to you to stay honest, I would suggest looking for another source.

I can subscribe to my county courthouse computer service. This may seem like a good idea, except that for some searches it will tell me only if there is a record and no more. Some computer files list most of the information, but still not everything that might be found in the physical file. Only about once a year would it really be nice for me to have just the limited information at my fingertips. I am close enough and can wait to get it the next day. This way I also know I am getting everything I can possibly get.

CRIMINAL RECORDS

Not everyone has a criminal record, but you would be surprised to find out how many people have been arrested and are now on file locally. In doing a search of criminal records, don't overlook the magistrate's office. Here you will find all of the lesser crimes, whereas the county courts only keep records of the more severe offenses. Previous arrest records can give you date of birth, Social Security number, description, address at the time of the offense, vehicles owned, and more, depending on the type of crime committed.

While we are talking about the criminal, don't overlook the obvious. More than once, when I was looking for someone and a criminal history started taking shape, the subject turned up in the county jail. If you get the feeling the person is in jail, don't just check your local jail—check those in surrounding counties or municipalities, too. Don't forget state and federal correctional systems, either. Your local telephone book will usually give you the numbers you need. If you're a good investigator, you'll find the numbers quickly.

CIVIL RECORDS

What a country! Everybody sues everybody at one time or another. That means there will be a record of the action somewhere. With that record, you will find out who hates whom, cheated whom, and fleeced whom. You will be surprised to find out just who has been sued in your community, why, and how many times.

When I first get a local case and happen to be downtown near the courthouse, I will do a civil search before anything else. Checking back just a few years usually doesn't take too long, and sometimes I will find out that someone else is looking for the subject. Maybe that person is willing to pay a few bucks to find the subject too; at the very least you can put someone in your debt. You never know when this new friend might come in handy as a source or for a favor.

For me, civil records also include recorded secured transactions and financial statements. Banks, financial institutions, and others that extend credit to individuals or companies and require these filings may be willing to help your subject. Most of the time when creditors hear someone is looking for one of their debtors, they will be willing to give information to find out if their investment is still safe. If you have information that might be helpful to them, they will want to hear about it. If you do give information back, be careful not to libel or slander yourself. You may want to offer in return a suggestion of where they might uncover damaging information on the subject, such as other creditors looking for the subject, closed back accounts, or other public records.

What you may also find is another business partner/debtor who may have the information you need. Why you are looking for someone may affect the way you question this person. If you are looking for a long-lost friend, you can be honest in your request for information. If you are looking for the person because you want to sue him for all he owns, a pretext or some verbal deception may be necessary. But you do not always have to resort to subterfuge to get information from such people. I know of several business people who will gladly give any and all information about their partners or

ex-partners, as the case may be. If your subject has done something to you that you don't like, it's probable he did the same to others.

When I talk about the courthouse, I am usually referring to the county courthouse, but remember, there are similar records in the state and federal courts. With the exception of the federal bankruptcy courts, I usually don't find it necessary to check these sources.

When I started out, like a lot of people, I was not aware of all that was in our local courthouse. I used to see a lot of people who were not employed by the county and who were not attorneys going in and out of the offices there. One day I walked into one of these offices when it wasn't too busy and asked the clerks just what kind of records they kept there and what all of these people were doing with them. That day I was lucky; the person I spoke to took the time to explain what all of the books and files were about. Meanwhile, I was thinking to myself, "How would this help me in my work as an investigator, especially in searching for missing persons?" From there I went to the next public office and did the same thing. Now I use the county courthouse for all it has to offer. You should too, as you should any government agency that deals with public records.

DEPARTMENT OF MOTOR VEHICLES

The motor vehicle department is probably the best-known and the most used resource for trying to locate someone. Most states have a procedure whereby you can get not only vehicle information, but operator information and history. Your local or state police can probably tell you what the procedure is; they may even have the necessary form for requesting the information. In some states you can get both operator and vehicle information by writing to the same address, while other states will require you to write to different addresses. Be forewarned, though, that when you request this information, you will go on record for having done so, which means the subject may become aware of it at some later date.

Requesting information from a government agency may subject you to certain laws of the land. Requesting certain information under an alias, for example, may be illegal. It is important to note here that if you use a fake name when requesting information from some government agencies, you will be signing legal documents. There is a time and place for pretexts and little white lies, but this is not one of them.

Most people would think checking whether the subject has an operator's license in the state would be sufficient to get them the information they want. The problem with this is that in most states the operator's license is only renewed every 4 years, which means the address on file might be almost 4 years old. A better record, if available, is the subject's vehicle registration. If he owns a vehicle, he must renew the registration every year, so chances are this address will be more current.

Most states require proof of insurance, and the DMV will have an insurance company on file somewhere. It may take a bit longer, but you can usually get this information. The same is true if there is an encumbrance on the vehicle. In this case, there will be a bank or someone else listed on the title who might know where the subject is or give you more information about him. Likewise, if the vehicle is leased, the leasing company may have some helpful information.

Most private investigators I know are honest and are known as such. Most have a friend or two at the police department who are willing to run checks on vehicles or names. The PI knows better than to abuse this favor. Some PIs will never use the local police, even though they have offered to provide the assistance. They feel it might compromise their case or obligate them to the police. If you have an association with a police officer who is willing to assist you in your search, all the better, but be sure not to abuse this privilege or misuse the information once you get it. Also, don't go bragging about the police officer who is helping you, especially not by name. It will get back to him or his superiors. You don't need that kind of trouble, nor does he.

LOCAL CONSTABLE AND SHERIFF'S OFFICES

There are times when I felt I have been very close to finding someone in some other community but just could not pin him down. The person you are looking for may have been the subject of someone else's civil complaint. A check with the local constable (if you have one) or sheriff's department may just tell you where he or she is. Here in Pennsylvania, the constables and sheriffs work within the court system as the ones who serve warrants, subpoenas, and complaints. Who better to know those who are in trouble the most or have the most reasons to be hunted? Their contacts within the community can at times make or break a case. Being a former constable myself, I know whereof I speak.

Since this is my book, I can brag a little, too. When I was a constable, as with any job, I tried to do the best I could. Most of my work involved serving criminal warrants for the district justices. They were not for America's most wanted, but they were still outstanding warrants that needed to be served. After several months, the number of new warrants from district justices was declining steadily. The word on the street was that people were turning themselves in. It seemed my reputation was starting to precede me. It may not have been by name, but the word on the street. There was finally a constable out there who hunted people, served warrants, and brought in criminals.

LOCAL POLICE

Like the constable and the sheriff's offices, the police usually have a good idea who is or is not in their community. Of course, the larger the community or city, the less true this is. Again, be forewarned—as with any law enforcement agency, the police do not have to cooperate with civilians. I have found, though, that usually when I tell them the reason I am looking for someone, I get a fair amount of information. There is only one way to find out, and that is to ask. The risk you are taking here—as with anytime you deal directly with people as sources—is the outside chance that the officer is friends with the subject and will tip him off. Obviously, if you are trying to find the subject without his knowing it, this is not good (just to let you know, since it has happened to me).

NEIGHBORHOOD BUSYBODY

This is the person you should love to meet when you're right out there hitting the streets, canvassing door to door. This person is always where the gossip is, taking it all in. He or she will tell you who is with whom, doing what, how big or small, when, why, and every other little thing you want to know about the community.

At first the busybodies may be hard to recognize, but you will soon learn to spot them. They usually start asking questions back with each one you ask. They will be the first to say they don't want to be nosy, but they are dying to hear all the details. Once you get them started, let them talk. You will, however, have to try to control the direction of the conversation, so as not to get too far off track from the information you are seeking. Chances are, if anybody knows what's going on in that community, they will. Sometimes you will have to hold out a carrot or make up something that will get them to reveal more because they want more from you. It may seem funny, bartering for information with the town's busybody, but it works. Why? Because these people love gossip—to hear it, then to tell it.

PRIVATE INVESTIGATORS

If you happen to be a PI, you know your bread and butter is information. If you go to a PI, he (or she) may already know something that will help you. You must be willing to pay something for what he has, whether monetarily or in kind. If what you ask for is not much, he may overlook this debt for now, but rest assured that it will be in the back of his mind. Someday, he may ask you for something in return. This is not to say all PIs are only looking out for number one. Think of it this way—how many full-time police officers or firemen would do their jobs if they were not getting paid? Most would still want to do the work but couldn't because they have financial responsibilities like everyone else. The same is true for the PI.

EMPLOYERS, PAST AND PRESENT

Depending on why you are looking for someone, if you know or find the current employer, your search could end right there. If you are trying to sneak up on someone, you may have to use pretexts to get the information out of the employer. Here again, entire books have been written on pretexts and how to use them. Sometimes, though, the direct approach works just as well. It's something you will have to decide when the situation arises.

Past employers will sometimes give you information; then again, they may not. There is only one way to find out, and that is to ask. I was looking for a bail jumper a number of years back and had learned who his past employer was. I called and asked if the person was still there. I was told that he had left several months ago. The personnel department at this company was very helpful, not only confirming the information I already had on the subject but proceeding to tell me things I didn't know. After that, I asked if they had a record of where the subject had relocated. At that time they did not, but they did tell me that they had received a call from a company checking on his past employment. With that, they gave me the name of the company, which turned out to be his current employer. We picked him up several days later at work.

If you are lucky enough to get employers, past or present, to talk to you, the information could take you to the subject's front door, or pretty darn close. If they give you references or tell you who they were instructed to notify in case of emergency, this can put you in touch with friends and family. You may be able to get a past address and previous employment. Former employers will probably have a record of the subject's education, which could lead you to an alumni association or a hometown. You can expect to get a Social Security number and, depending on the job, a driver's license number for your subject. You may find out the subject was bonded, or that he had a special training certification that must be renewed periodically.

There is no doubt that former employers can be among the most valuable sources of information. Think of how much you divulged to your employer when you applied for your job. Think of what you revealed about yourself, above and beyond what you put on your application or résumé. Chances are that if you were to look in the file your employer has on you (if you are not self-employed), you would be very surprised to learn how much he knows about you. Who knows, maybe he even hired someone like me to do an employment check on you.

TELEPHONE RECORDS

Depending on your client, telephone records may or may not be available to you. If you are looking for a teenage runaway, checking the family phone records is a must. If the phone records belong to someone else, most of the time you're out of luck, unless you happen to be in law enforcement and your department has a good working relationship with the telephone company. Most private citizens have no legal way to get a copy of someone else's phone records. Like other PIs, I get advertisements in the mail all the time about how a certain company can get telephone records for me. I have a good idea of how they do this, but I will not discuss that here. Again, there are other books written that will tell you how to trick the phone company into giving you these records.

I knew a fellow who used to get telephone records all the time for his work in repossessing cars, and it worked very well for him. First, he would call someone in the subject's family with a story that would cause the relative to call the subject right after they were finished talking. He would then get the telephone records to see what number the relative called just after hanging up. Sometimes it worked, but as when using other fringe sources, you must ask yourself if you are willing to pay the price for what you want. These sources are not only expensive and questionable, but the civil liability can be immeasurable.

DATA BANKS AND CREDIT BUREAUS

I mentioned data banks earlier with regard to cross-referencing services, but data banks and credit bureaus do more than just that. If you have a Social Security number for your subject, some auxiliary services can bring up his or her last known address on the system for you. Rather than joining a credit bureau, you may be able to get someone who is already a member to obtain reports for you as needed, but this does put your source at risk for any and all abuses on your part. If you choose to use the services of a credit bureau, directly or indirectly, you must follow the rules set forth by the Fair Credit Reporting Act. If you deal with the bureau directly as a member, it will help to keep you honest.

If you are using the service of a private company that acts as a middle man for the credit bureaus or one of the major credit reporting agencies, be careful. Some—and I emphasize only *some*—will hint that they can get or do almost anything. These same companies will then tell you not to worry about the legality of it, because people hardly ever get caught misusing the system, and if they do, nothing happens anyway. Don't you believe it! Recently, a detective agency was fined heavily for abusing the system. In some states, such an offense could cost you your license. They will still make you sign all the papers, stating that you will follow all of the rules. In the end, all they want is for you to keep sending them money, no matter how you use the system. There are not many companies like this, but be forewarned, there are some out there.

LIBRARIES

Probably the most overlooked source of information is the library. Whether public, private, or in a high school or college, consider the library one of your most powerful sources of information. I know of investigators who have probably not been in a library since high school. Since what you are looking for is information, there is no better place to look. We have an excellent local library, and I am only an hour away from our state library. I use them both frequently. The following list contains just a few examples of the kinds of books you can expect to find in the reference section of your local public library:

- Cross-reference directories
- *Who's Who* listings
- Directories of clubs and associations
- Atlases
- Local, county, state, and federal government directories
- Directories of data banks
- Directories of major businesses

Again, this list is just the beginning. If you go into the library, you will probably find a few more sources that will spark your interest. If you look hard and start going through the regular stacks, you might even find another book on how to find missing persons.

Just as an aside, in my personal library I have hundreds of books. Many are just plain reference books and different kinds of directories. As I've already mentioned, this includes a large collection of telephone directories for cities in my state and other major cities across the country. The joke in our family is that if you need information on something, go see Uncle Roger, because he probably has the book on what you need. On the serious side, I do value books and what they can do for you. I frequent bookstores, new and used. I get book catalogs from a number of different companies. In Appendix F I have listed several companies that deal with books on investigation and related services. Be forewarned that some of them advertise books that are not for everyone, but I am sure you will find something you like. That's what freedom of the press is all about.

SOCIAL SECURITY ADMINISTRATION

First and foremost, the Social Security Administration (SSA) will not tell you where the subject is. It does have a heart, though. If you have a legitimate and honorable reason for hunting someone, such as finding parents, children, or other close relatives, it will help you. What you need to do is write a letter to the subject and send it to the SSA with as much information as possible identifying your subject (obviously, a Social Security number would be a great thing to have in this case). The SSA will then forward the letter to the subject's last known address, and then it will be up to the subject to get back to you. To find out more about this service, contact your local Social Security Administration office or write to: Social Security Administration, Public Inquiries, Dept. of Health and Human Services, 6401 Security Blvd., Baltimore, MD 21235, or call (301) 594-5970.

I once had an attorney tell me he had planned to call me to help find the long-lost father of one of his clients, but he said he had heard of this service and wanted to try it first. It took awhile, but the father did eventually call the client. I didn't make any money, but he found the person he was looking for.

CHAPTER FIVE

THINGS TO THINK ABOUT

The purpose of your investigation is to find someone. You do that by having the right information. To get the information from people, you must ask questions, and when you are tired of that, ask more. By asking the questions in a slightly different way, you may spark something they had forgotten. When they do start talking, let them talk unless they start getting too far off track. When they stop talking, wait just a few seconds before you ask your next question. Many people are uncomfortable with silence in the middle of a conversation. Because of that, the person is likely to start talking again and giving you more details—details that might be important clues to the answer to the question you just asked.

How many times have you finished talking to people and then remembered something you wanted to tell them after they were gone? The same thing can happen with the people you interview. Leave a business card or your telephone number with them so that they can get back to you if they think of something new. While it may not be too often, it does happen. I find that it often happens after I've found the person I'm looking for, but there have been a few times when it did help me locate subjects, too.

How's your memory? If you don't have a good memory, write

things down as you talk to someone. Carry a tape recorder if you have to, but get the details. I cannot stress that enough. The small, important details can make or break a case. What are the small, important details? It's hard to give specific examples, but given time, you will start to learn what to pick out. What you have to do is to go out there and get your feet wet.

My memory isn't too bad, but my handwriting is so bad I should be a doctor. No, I should be a brain surgeon. My second fault is that I cannot spell worth a darn. Can you imagine what my notes look like? Okay, maybe they do look like hieroglyphics, but I can read them—most of the time. The point here is, keep fixing your notes as you go along. Be careful of what your client tells you from his notes. His handwriting may be just as bad as mine, and maybe he can't read it himself. He may be giving you bad information unintentionally. Look for variations in spelling when you are doing your work. Maybe you are a good speller and he's not. If you keep working with the wrong name, you probably aren't going to get too far. If you keep an open mind as you go along and watch the name for slightly different spellings, you might just hit the target. Be on the lookout not just for your mistakes but those of your clients as well.

Not only can you misspell something, but numbers have a bad habit of getting mixed up too. Watch the numbers you write down, and recheck them with other sources as you go along. Mixed-up driver's license numbers or Social Security numbers will do nothing but drive you crazy. When your sources start telling you that your subject doesn't exist in conjunction with a number, you start wondering if he or she really exists at all. One quick cure for bad handwriting and poor spelling is a roll of quarters. With a pocket of quarters, I can become the greatest speller since Webster (and I don't get as many parking tickets, either). By placing a quarter in the slot of the court-house copy machine, I ensure that I never misspell a name or write down a wrong number again. If it's wrong, it's because someone else typed it wrong on the file or record. Why, with so much to write down, would you want to practice your penmanship when the copy machine is over there in the corner?

Since we are on the subject of files, these things contain some of the most boring reading ever. Lawyers just love to add words to everything and anything they can get their hands on. But rest assured, in the files that are the thickest, chances are you will find some diamonds. It may take awhile, but it is well worth the search. I have found a number of gems in the garbage I've gone through.

CHAPTER SIX

WHEN YOU ARE STUMPED

It doesn't matter how long you've been in the business of hunting people, eventually you will be stopped dead. You will have checked and rechecked all of your sources, and still you will be no closer to finding the subject than you were weeks earlier. First, you must realize that there are going to be some people neither you nor any other investigator can find. Even if you had unlimited funds, they still probably could not be found. When looking for missing persons, it's important to keep cost-effectiveness in mind. It just doesn't pay to spend thousands of dollars to find someone who skipped on a $600 loan. When hunting a relative or a lost love, it may be that you want to spend whatever it takes but just don't have the money to go that far. So if you need to continue, what do you do?

If the case must be worked, swallow your pride and give it to someone else. If you cannot do that, read off what you have with someone else who might think of something you didn't. In the past, our local group of investigators has brainstormed on cases that had one of us stumped. Though we represent different agencies, we have a great working relationship. Maybe you have someone you can brainstorm with. If not, what else can you do?

The first thing you do is absolutely nothing. Get away from the case and take a rest from it. Many times an amazing thing will start happening several days or weeks later. Out of nowhere, you will be hit with an idea about what to do next. This will be a bit off the wall for some of you, but when you put the case out of your conscious mind, the subconscious mind takes over. Your subconscious mind just loves to do this kind of thing, as it is much more imaginative than your conscious mind—and less inhibited, too. It's like your dreams. Could you possibly think up all that weird stuff you dream? Let the really creative part of your brain take over for awhile. Then, when you least expect it, a solution will jump out at you and scream, "I got it!" (At least it works for me.)

If this doesn't work for you or it doesn't work soon enough, you still have to get away from the case for awhile. Then, after several weeks, if you can afford to be away from it for that long, pick up your case file again. But instead of opening it and picking up where you left off, the best thing to do is to give the file a good heave in the air. You may be thinking about now that this PI is really losing it. Not so. What is the next thing you have to do? You have to pick up the whole mess.

This is where this technique works. As you start putting things back in the file, you start looking at what you have in a different way. At the same time, start rewriting some of your notes. Soon something nice will start to happen. New ideas will start coming into your head. Think of it this way. Imagine that you are putting together a puzzle with some pieces that are shaped the same. The picture you are getting isn't becoming clear, and you have used up all of your pieces. What happens when you mix them all up and start over again? This time, looking at it a different way, you might get it right. This worked for me once when I was stumped on an adoption case that I was working on for more than three months. When I was putting the pieces back together an idea hit me, and I checked out a name in a slightly different way. Within minutes, I was talking to the client's natural father, who in turn gave me the mother's full name, address, and telephone number.

CHAPTER SEVEN

COINCIDENCES DO HAPPEN!

If you keep your eyes and ears open, sometimes you just get plain lucky. About 4 years ago I was involved in a murder defense case. I was working with another PI who was highly respected for his expertise on these types of cases. He had asked me to work with him in locating more than 30 people who were connected in one way or another to the case.

The case spanned a three-county area, and we worked it solid for almost a month. When it was all said and done, we located and interviewed all but one person on our original list. We also added about 10 new people who were not known to the defense counsel and were important to the case. When the case was over I went back to my regular caseload.

About a month later, a law firm in an adjoining county called. It needed me to locate a man and serve a subpoena on him as soon as possible. They said it might be difficult because all they had on the subject was a rural route box number. It was late afternoon, and I knew the post office would be closed by the time I got there. Sometimes by calling the post office you can find out where the person lives, but only if that route carrier happens to be there. It wasn't likely he would be. I drove over to the law firm right away to pick up the subpoena and read the name and address. I smiled on the inside and told them that it may be tough, but I would get it done. When I looked at the subpoena, I recognized the subject right away as one of the people I had located and interviewed about a month earlier. I even remembered his working hours and knew he would probably be home very soon. It didn't take me more than an hour to do the job. I probably spent more time going to and from the attorney's office than I did serving the subpoena. Coincidences do happen. Take them and have fun.

More recently, an attorney asked me to be prepared to swear that an individual was still around town but just avoiding his obligation to appear in court. I had served the subject several weeks prior to this, at which time he had stated that he was moving out of state and was not going to show up. He made it clear he did not want to testify.

The subject's court date to register as a witness came and went, and he never showed up. The trial was about a day away, and we still weren't sure he was in town. I went back to his residence, his place of work, and all of his hangouts. Still, while there were some rumors that he was still in town, I hadn't seen him. Finally, on the day of the trial, I was taking my report to the attorney and I had still not seen the subject since I first served the subpoena on him. On the way, I turned onto the street in front of the courthouse and spotted a familiar vehicle. I pulled up alongside it and gave the subject a friendly smile and a wave. He was not happy to see me. I went up to the attorney's office, had a staff member type up a brief supplement to my report, and put my signature on it. Keep your eyes open; you never know whom you might run into.

CHAPTER EIGHT

STATE OF MIND

Though I don't like to classify them as sources, some everyday people help me, too. I don't use people and then discard them; they are too valuable as friends to do that. But at times, when it is necessary, I do ask for their help. If I go to a past client who I think might have information that will help me in a case, 99 percent of the time, the person will tell me what I want without ever asking why. I look to my friends who might have particular knowledge about something or someone, as long as it does not jeopardize them. It's surprising how much members of your family know that might help you, too. On one case, I had to go back to my hometown. The first person I talked to was my mother, asking her what she knew of the situation.

Networking is an important part of what I do. Information comes from people. Sometimes you can only get the information if you know someone who is part of a special group. You cannot be the best investigator possible if you're a hermit. Not to sound mercenary, but when you meet someone for the first time, you must think how just knowing this person might help you do a better job of finding people. Remember, though, these people are important to you, but not just because you need them. They are important, period. Never let yourself forget it. It's a good idea to let them know how important they are to you and how much you appreciate it.

This brings up another point. Obviously, when you are dealing with public records, you have to deal with public employees. This is not meant to slander them but rather to help you in your quest for information. The fact is that they have control over something you want to see. They can make it easy or almost impossible to get the information you need. Even the seasoned investigator will find that a disgruntled public servant can make a job take ten to a hundred times longer. This is the exception and not the rule. In many of the local courthouses in my area, I am somewhat known and receive the utmost in help, courtesy, and assistance.

It should go without saying that anytime you receive any small assistance, a thank-you is in order. Saying please is still considered polite. Like most other people, the people who help you want to feel that what they do is important and appreciated. There are probably a hundred clichés about how you can get more from people by treating them nicely rather than being abusive. If this is one of your shortcomings, I highly recommend reading Dale Carnegie's book, *How to Win Friends and Influence People*, or listening to it on cassette tape. Better yet, if you have the time and money, enroll in one of the Dale Carnegie courses. The "Effective Speaking and Human Relations" course is well known around the world. There are plenty of other good personal-development training companies out there, but the Carnegie courses are some of the best known. Again, if you need help in this area, getting it will help you not only in your work, but in your personal life, too. It is worth the time and money.

I cannot count the times I have asked for help, and once I explained to the person I was asking how important my particular case was, and how his or her help was important, too, that person would bend over backwards and do half the work for me. Sometimes you may get more than you really should, and in some cases that is a big help.

Sometimes, though, you will meet the confrontational type of employee. At times, this person can be the most frustrating obstacle you will ever encounter. You know he has what you want. You know you are entitled to the information he has and that he will do everything in his power to keep you from getting it or getting it in a reasonable amount of time. The first thing you can do is refrain from becoming bitter and angry with him. You must recognize that this is probably the only area in his whole world where he has any control or power. This is where he can be a dictator—many times unchecked and unchallenged. When you recognize what a little person this type of public employee really is, you will find it easier to manage the situation.

When you know that you are entitled to the information and the person is stalling deliberately, it's time to play hardball. In a calm but authoritative tone, you tell this employee that you know you are entitled to the information. If you can quote certain legal statutes, all the better. Tell him that if you do not start getting cooperation soon, you will see his supervisor. If he really seems uncooperative and claims he is in charge, remind him that there is always someone higher. Inform him that you have several options in going over his head and that you will not hesitate to file a written complaint against him, his supervisor, and anyone else you see as necessary. Inform him that you will even go as high as the elected official in that branch of government if need be. By this time you should start seeing some results.

Still you may find the one real hardnose who still will not budge.

In this case, you might follow through with your threats. If you cannot get the information by other means and it is that important to you, filing civil action may be necessary. I sincerely hope you don't have to go this far to get what you need.

CONCLUSION

So now that you have read all of this, are you ready to try and find Jimmy Hoffa? If so, good luck, because that's probably the only way he will be found. But if you're ready to try and find an old friend or an old SOB who still owes you a few bucks, you're now prepared to begin your hunt. Even though I have given you this information here, the one thing you will have to get on your own is experience.

I have told a few stories that I hope will help put you in the state of mind to think like an investigator. I listed a number of my favorite sources that work for you. Like anything, the more you do something, the better you will become at doing it.

When I first started in the trade, I really didn't know where to begin. I was guided by my friend in the business. Later, through some self-discovery, I began to think like an investigator. After you do your first investigation, you will start to "get the feel of the road" in being a missing persons investigator. When you do your second search, you will probably find that another source of information will be better to use than the source you used in your first one. In your third investigation, you may find out it isn't as easy as it looks. It may take a bit longer. It may even take a lot longer, but you will be getting the experience necessary to become a better investigator.

If you are really fortunate, you may find an investigator who will let you be an apprentice. This may be in the form of being a gofer or clerk. You may have to do some unpleasant or tedious work before you even get close to a real case. But if you do what you're supposed to do, you can watch and learn from the pros as they do their work. Eventually, you will be given small assignments with instructions as to what to do. Later, you will probably be told to handle a case, but with much more leeway to try and figure it out for yourself, although still within certain limits. This is probably the most ideal way of learning this trade. If it happens to you, consider yourself very fortunate.

Your personal library will become larger with other investigations and reference books. If you continue to do more manhunting, you will probably spend some money on seminars or classes on investigation at your local college if they have a Police Science curriculum. Your search for more information and knowledge should not be limited by what you read here. As I told you in the beginning of this book, there are a lot of other books out there on this subject. One consideration I always keep in mind about buying books is that if I get just one new idea that will help me with my work, the book was probably worth the money.

Later, not only will you become better at finding people, but you will discover ways that are quicker than when you first started. You will learn to reduce the actual legwork involved and become more proficient in using the telephone. As you progress, you will learn to save both time and money.

If your work requires you to look for people, such as being a credit manager looking for debtors or a paralegal looking for witnesses, and you have now successfully started to find people, you will probably be bitten by the "private detective" bug. If so, watch out. Once you get it, it's hard to shake. You'll start looking in the Yellow Pages for who's listed under detective or investigation agencies. You'll probably start driving by their offices, thinking maybe you should go in and see if you could start working for them part-time. You may even think about getting your own PI license. When you buy a fedora hat and trench coat, then you have the bug really bad. If this happens to you, enjoy the feeling and follow your instincts. Maybe a career change is meant to be. Then again, maybe not. But if nothing else, you will get a taste of what many people only dream about.

MISSING PERSON REPORT, PERSONAL DATA

NAME: _____
            Last   First   Middle

ADDRESS: _____
        Street   City   State   Zip

PHONE: _____ D.O.B.: _____ SEX: _____

OCCUPATION: _____ EMPLOYER: _____

SS#: _____ ALIAS: _____

U.S. CITIZEN: _____ NATIVE BORN OR NATURALIZED: _____

NATIVE COUNTRY: _____

EMPLOYER ADDRESS: _____

HOW LONG: _____ WORK PHONE: _____

POSSIBLE DESTINATION: _____

POSSIBLE CAUSE OF ABSENCE: _____

TIME & DATE LAST SEEN: _____

LAST SEEN AT: _____

VEHICLE: _____
     Make   Model   Year   Color   Doors

TAG AND STATE REG. _____ CONDITION: _____

OPERATOR'S LICENSE #: _____ TYPE: _____

DRIVING RECORD (accidents, citations, suspensions): _____

_____

VEHICLE OWNER: _____

OWNER'S ADDRESS: _____

AUTO INSURANCE CO.: _____

INS. CO. ADDRESS: _____ PHONE: _____

ENCUMBRANCE: _____ TO WHOM: _____

SUBJECT'S PHYSICAL DESCRIPTION

HEIGHT: _____ WEIGHT: _____ BUILD: _____

EYES: _____ GLASSES: _____ CONTACT LENSES: _____

HAIR COLOR: _____ LENGTH OR STYLE: _____

PART (side, middle, none): _____ SIDEBURNS: _____

MOUSTACHE: _____ BEARD: _____

TEETH (condition, any missing): _____

EARS (earrings): _____

COMPLEXION: _____ EYEBROWS: _____

VOCAL TRAITS OR ACCENTS: _____

SCARS OR DEFORMITIES: _____

TATTOOS: _____

BIRTHMARKS: _____ MOLES: _____

CONDITION (Mental): _____

(Physical): _____

MISSING PERSON REPORT, PERSONAL DATA

UNDER DOCTOR'S CARE: _____ DOCTOR'S NAME: _____

DOCTOR'S ADDRESS: _____

SPECIAL DIETARY NEEDS: _____

SPECIAL MEDICATION: _____

RIGHT- OR LEFT-HANDED: _____ RINGS: _____

SMOKER: _____ DRINKER: _____ DRUG ABUSER: _____

OTHER VICES: _____

CONSPICUOUS CHARACTERISTICS, HABITS, OR MANNERISMS: _____

_____

_____

_____

NIGHTCLUBS OR HANGOUTS FREQUENTED: _____

_____

CLOTHING (last seen wearing): _____

_____

JEWELRY: _____

CLOTHING TAKEN: _____

_____

_____

BRIEFCASE OR HANDBAG: _____ MONEY ON PERSON: _____

PAWNABLE ITEMS TAKEN: _____

_____

PHOTOGRAPH AVAILABLE: _____ DATE OF PHOTO: _____

CLOSE FRIENDS: _____

_____

_____

PERSONAL HISTORY

PLACE OF BIRTH: _____

                       City   State   Country

FATHER'S NAME: _____ D.O.B.: _____

ADDRESS: _____

FATHER'S HOMETOWN: _____ OCCUPATION: _____

EMPLOYER & ADDRESS: _____

MOTHER'S NAME (Maiden): _____ D.O.B.: _____

ADDRESS: _____

MOTHER'S HOMETOWN: _____ OCCUPATION: _____

EMPLOYER & ADDRESS: _____

BROTHERS & SISTERS (names, addresses, D.O.B., occupations): _____

_____

_____

_____

_____

OTHER RELATIVES: _____

_____

MISSING PERSON REPORT, PERSONAL DATA

SPOUSE'S NAME: _____ D.O.B.: _____

ADDRESS: _____

SPOUSE'S HOMETOWN: _____ OCCUPATION: _____

EMPLOYER & ADDRESS: _____

CHILDREN (names, addresses, D.O.B.s, occupations): _____

_____

_____

_____

DIVORCED: _____ WHERE FILED: _____

FORMER SPOUSE: _____ D.O.B.: _____

ADDRESS: _____

EMPLOYER & ADDRESS: _____

ALIMONY/SUPPORT: $ _____ HOW SENT: _____

HOW RECENT & HOW OFTEN: _____

SUBJECT'S FORMER OCCUPATIONS/EMPLOYERS & ADDRESSES: _____

_____

_____

_____

FRIENDS (addresses): _____

_____

_____

_____

GRADE SCHOOL & ADDRESS: _____

HIGH SCHOOL & ADDRESS: _____

COLLEGE & ADDRESS: _____

DEGREE: _____ YEAR GRADUATED: _____

OTHER SCHOOLS ATTENDED: _____

_____

FAVORITE VACATION SPOTS: _____

_____

PAST ADDRESSES: _____

_____

_____

_____

P.O. BOX: _____ CITY: _____

HOBBIES & CLUBS: _____

_____

_____

FINANCIAL

BANK: _____ BRANCH: _____

ADDRESS: _____

CHECKING ACCOUNT NUMBER: _____ BALANCE: $ _____

SAVINGS ACCOUNT NUMBER: _____ BALANCE: $ _____

ANY MONIES REMOVED FROM ANY ACCOUNTS: _____

MISSING PERSON REPORT, PERSONAL DATA

CONTENTS OF SAFE-DEPOSIT BOX: _____

_____

_____

OTHER BANKS: _____

_____

_____

STOCKBROKER: _____

ADDRESS: _____

CREDIT CARDS: _____

_____

_____

PEOPLE WHO OWE MONEY TO SUBJECT: _____

_____

_____

ON UNEMPLOYMENT: _____ HOW LONG: _____

ATTORNEY: _____

ADDRESS: _____

REAL ESTATE AGENT: _____

ADDRESS: _____

PENSION OR RETIREMENT FUND: _____

OTHER INCOME: _____

OTHER PROPERTIES OWNED: _____

FINGERPRINTED: _____ WHEN: _____ WHERE: _____

REASON: _____

POLICE RECORD: _____ WHERE: _____

CHARGES AND DISPOSITIONS: _____

_____

_____

_____

PRISON: _____ DATES SERVED: _____

PAROLE OFFICER: _____

PAROLE OFFICE & ADDRESS: _____

OUTSTANDING WARRANTS: _____

MENTAL HOSPITALS: _____

WEAPONS PERMIT: _____ WHERE: _____

MAKE: _____ CAL.: _____ SER.#: _____

MAKE: _____ CAL.: _____ SER.#: _____

OTHER WEAPONS: _____

OUTSTANDING CIVIL SUITS: _____

_____

ANYONE ELSE LOOKING FOR SUBJECT & WHY: _____

_____

PASSPORT: _____ VISAS: _____

LAUNDRY MARKS OR CLEANING MARKS: _____

PETS: _____

VETERINARIAN: _____

HUNTING/FISHING LICENSES: _____

ARMED FORCES BRANCH: _____

UNIT: _____ LOC. OF LAST ASSIGNED DUTY: _____

DATE IN: _____ DATE OUT: _____ RANK: _____

WHERE DISCHARGED: _____

VETERAN'S ORGANIZATIONS: _____

_____

REGISTERED VOTER: _____ WHERE: _____

UNION OR TRADE ORGANIZATIONS: _____

_____

P.O. FORWARDING: _____

MISCELLANEOUS

WHERE DOES CLIENT THINK THE SUBJECT IS? _____

EXPLANATION: _____

_____

HAS ANY FRIEND OR RELATIVE BEEN CONTACTED? _____

_____

POSSIBLE CONTACTS: _____

AUTHORITIES NOTIFIED: _____

PREVIOUSLY MISSING: _____ WHEN: _____ HOW LONG: _____

CIRCUMSTANCES: _____

_____

_____

_____

WILL CLIENT ACCEPT ALL COLLECT CALLS? _____

CLIENT: _____

ADDRESS: _____
_____City_____State_____Zip_____

HOME PHONE: _____ WORK PHONE: _____

REFERRED BY: _____

NOTES: _____

_____

_____

_____

_____

_____

INTERVIEWED BY: _____ DATE: _____

REQUEST FOR CHANGE OF ADDRESS

Postmaster,   (date)

    I, _____, am requesting information on the current postal address of _____ .

    The last known address of this person, known to this office, is _____. Please check the status on this person listed at this address. As required, enclosed is a check ($3 per request) for providing this service. Please feel free to answer this letter by filling in the appropriate information below. Your help and immediate attention to this matter are greatly appreciated.

                                  Sincerely,

                                  (Signed)

                                  (Return address if not on letterhead)

❑ Current address is good as shown.

❑ Moved with no forwarding address.

❑ No record found on that person.

❑ Moved with the forwarding address of:

_____

_____

_____

Date moved _____

REQUEST FOR P.O. BOX DISCLOSURE

Postmaster,   (date)

I, ——————————————— , am requesting the address of
——————————————— , holder of P.O. Box ——— in the city of
——————————————— , State ——————— Zip ——————— .
Pursuant to Postal Service Regulation, Administrative Support Manual, Section 352.44f(2), I do hearby certify that litigation has commenced or will soon commence and the address information is necessary to effect service of court process upon said boxholder and for no other purpose.

By virtue of Section ——————— , Rule ——————— , in the county of
——————————————— , in the state of ——————————————— , I am lawfully empowered to serve process.

Names of all known parties: ———————————————
Court of: ———————————————
Case or Docket Number: ———————————————
The boxholder is served in the capacity of being a:

❑ defendant

❑ witness

❑ other ———————————————

Sincerely,

(Signed)

(Return address if not on letterhead)

REQUEST FOR BUSINESS P.O. BOX HOLDER INFORMATION

Postmaster,   (date)

I, —————————————————————— , am requesting the street address of —————————————————————— , holder of P.O. Box ——————— , City——————————————— , State ——————— Zip ——————— , pursuant to the provisions of Postal Service Regulations, Administrative Support Manual, Section 352.44e(l). The reason for this request is that said boxholder is conducting a business known as ——————————————————— through the listed post office box, and that I, as a customer, require his street in order to pursue a complaint with the company listed above.

Sincerely,

(Signed)

(Return address if not on letterhead)

MILITARY LOCATOR ADDRESSES

Air Force

AF MPC/MPC D003

9504 IH 35N

San Antonio, TX 78233-6636

512-652-5774

Army

USAEREC

ATTN: Locator Branch

Ft. Harrison, IN 46249-5301

317-542-3647

Marine Corps

CMC MMRB-10

HQ U.S. Marine Corps

Washington, D.C. 20380

202-694-1851

Navy

Naval Military Personnel

Command N 036cc

Washington, D.C. 20370-5036

202-694-3155

BOOK DISTRIBUTORS AND PUBLISHERS

Butterworth Publishers
80 Montvale Avenue
Stoneham, MA 02180

Delta Press Ltd.
215 South Washington Street
P.O. Box 1625
El Dorado, AR 71731

Eden Press, Inc.
P.O. Box 8410
Fountain Valley, CA 92728

Loompanic Unlimited Publishers
P.O. Box 1197
Port Townsend, WA 98368

NIC, Inc. Law Enforcement Supply
220 Carroll Street, Suite D
P.O. Box 5950
Shreveport, LA 71135-5950

Nightingale-Conant Corporation
7100 North Lehigh Avenue
Niles, IL 60714

Paladin Press
P.O. Box 1307
Boulder, CO 80306

Survival Books
11106 Magnolia Blvd.
North Hollywood, CA 91601-3810

Thomas Publications
P.O. Box 33244
Austin, TX 78764

BIBLIOGRAPHY

Akin, Richard H. *The Private Investigator's Basic Manual.* Springfield, IL: Charles C. Thomas, 1979.

Blye, Irwin, and Ardy Friedberg. *Secrets of a Private Eye.* New York: Henry Holt and Company, 1987.

Carnegie, Dale. *How to Win Friends and Influence People.* New York: Simon & Schuster, 1981.

Carroll, John M. *Confidential Information Sources: Public & Private.* Stoneham, MA: Butterworth Publishers, Inc., 1975.

Faron, Fay. *Take the Money and Strut.* San Francisco: Zero to Sixty Pubco, 1983.

Goldfader, Ed. *Tracer! The Search for Missing Persons.* Los Angeles: Nash Publishing, 1970.

Lapin, Lee. *How to Get Anything on Anybody.* Boulder, CO: Paladin Press, 1987.

Lapin, Lee. *How to Get Anything on Anybody: Book II.* San Mateo, CA: ISECO, Inc., 1991.

Lesko, Matthew. *Information U.S.A.* New York: Viking and Penguin Books, 1986.

Makower, Joel and Alan Green. *Instant Information.* New York: Tidlen Press, Prentice Hall, 1987.

McCann, John. *Find 'Em Fast.* Boulder, CO: Paladin Press, 1984.

O'Hara, Charles E. *Fundamentals of Criminal Investigation.* Springfield, IL: Charles C. Thomas, 1970.

Pryor, Bill. *Secret Agent, Vol. 1*. Fountain Valley, CA: Eden Press, 1986.

Sherick, L.C. *How to Use the Freedom of Information Act (FOIA)*. New York: Arco Publishing Company, 1978.

Thomas, Ralph D. *1027 Secret Sources and Techniques for Locating Missing Persons*. Austin, TX: Thomas Publications, 1983.